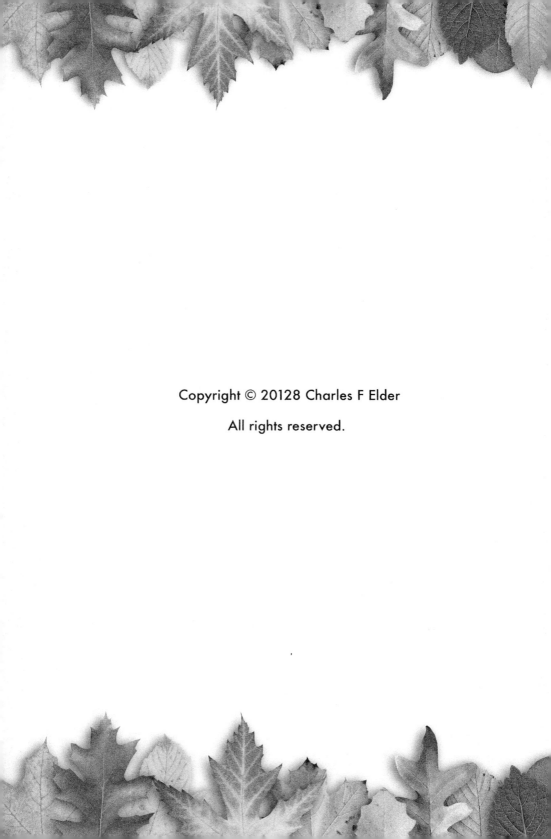

Copyright © 20128 Charles F Elder

All rights reserved.

Gatherer

A Forager's journal with logs and blank pages to record your find with helpful monthly recipes to give you some inspiration!

DISCLAIMER

The information in this journal is not intended or implied to be a substitute for professional medical advice, diagnosis or treatment. This Journal is intended to provide general information only.

Do not eat any wild edible plants, herbs, weeds, trees or bushes until you have verified with your health professional that they are safe for you.

Keep all plants away from children. As with any natural product, they can be toxic if misused.

SAFETY AND CONSIDERATION

Safety
Please do not pick anything unless you are 110% sure of your ability to correctly identify the plant, I have included some common plants in the recipes that most people should be familiar with, but if in doubt... don't eat it, I found joining some foraging walks very helpful and great fun.

Avoid plants near farmers fields around spraying time and plants close to the main roads as some can absorb the pollution.

Consideration
If you can't see at least ten of the plants you plan to harvest and you know it is not a very common plant like nettles for example, please do not harvest it, also leave some of the flower for the birds and insects only pick a percentage of the berries or flowers from each bush or tree.

Cooking Conversions

Measurements

Cup	Ounces	Millilitres	Grams
8	64	1895	1814
6	48	1420	1360
5	40	1180	1133
4	32	960	907
2	16	480	453
1	8	240	226
3/4	6	177	170
2/4	5	158	141
1/2	4	118	113
3/8	3	90	85
1/3	2.5	79	70
1/4	2	59	56
1/8	1	30	28
1/16	1/2	15	14

Quercus

EK, QUERCUS ROBUR L.

JANUARY

Roasted Chilly Acorns
Quercus

Random fact
Wine corks come from the Cork
Oak *Quercus suber*.

Harvest
Collect into bags after they have fallen.

Checking that they all look "fresh" and
that there are no black holes.

Freeze overnight in freezer and then shell.
The freezing makes this easier to shell.

Soak in boiling water and repeat
until water is clear.

This removes the tannins.

JANUARY

Method

Sprinkle with salt and chilly flakes.

Put on a baking tray on a high heat until brown (around 20mins)

Serve up with a cask ale
Buon appetito!

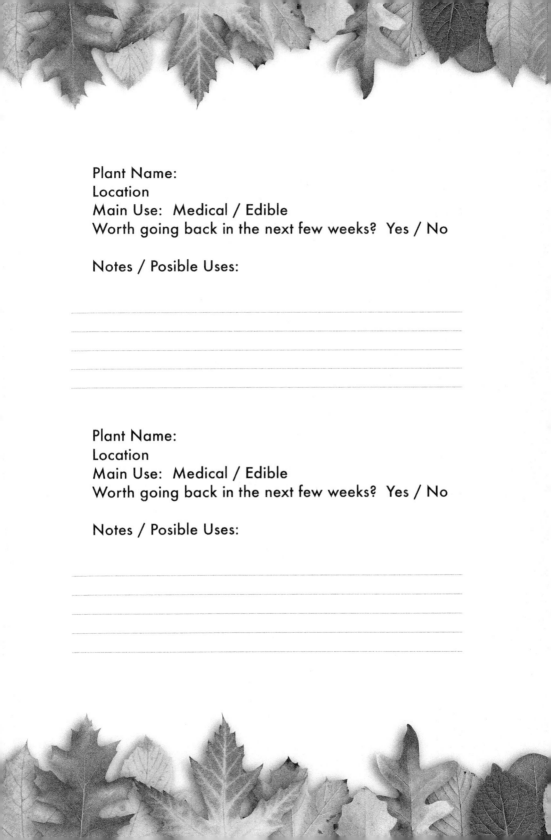

Plant Name:
Location
Main Use: Medical / Edible
Worth going back in the next few weeks? Yes / No

Notes / Posible Uses:

Plant Name:
Location
Main Use: Medical / Edible
Worth going back in the next few weeks? Yes / No

Notes / Posible Uses:

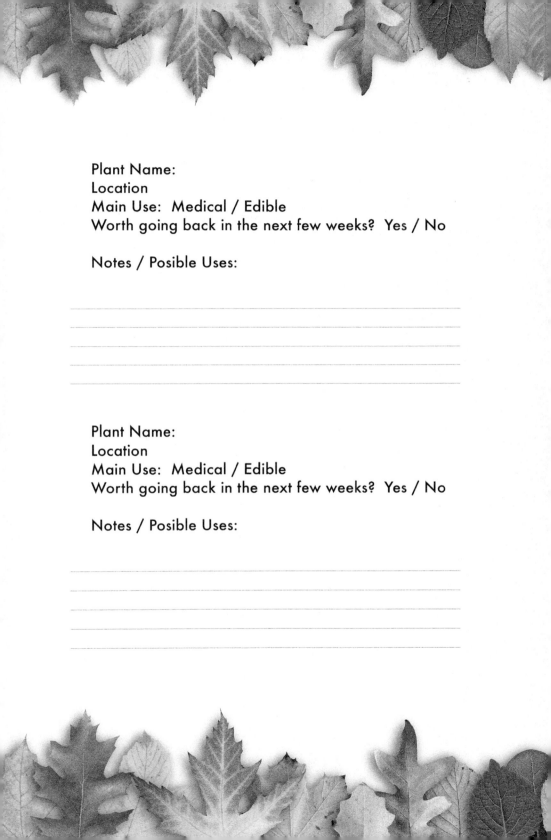

Plant Name:
Location
Main Use: Medical / Edible
Worth going back in the next few weeks? Yes / No

Notes / Posible Uses:

———————————————————————————
———————————————————————————
———————————————————————————
———————————————————————————
———————————————————————————

Plant Name:
Location
Main Use: Medical / Edible
Worth going back in the next few weeks? Yes / No

Notes / Posible Uses:

———————————————————————————
———————————————————————————
———————————————————————————
———————————————————————————
———————————————————————————

Plant Name:
Location
Main Use: Medical / Edible
Worth going back in the next few weeks? Yes / No

Notes / Posible Uses:

_____
_____
_____
_____
_____

Plant Name:
Location
Main Use: Medical / Edible
Worth going back in the next few weeks? Yes / No

Notes / Posible Uses:

_____
_____
_____
_____
_____

Stellaria Media

A. GRÄSSTJÄRNBLOMMA, STELLARIA GRAMINEA L.
B. VÅTARV, STELLARIA MEDIA CYR.

FEBRUARY

Chickweed pesto on pasta
Stellaria Media

Random fact
Stellaria in the latin name refers to the small white star like flowers

Harvest
Make sure you have the right plant.

Check that hairs are running only along one side of the stem.

Chickweed's stems, leaves, flowers and seeds are all edible.

Ingredients
Olive Oil
Garlic
Nuts
Hard Cheese

FEBRUARY

Method
Add chickweed to blender and
blend with a hard cheese and garlic.

Add some type of nut, maybe
any surviving acorns from last month
or if not some walnuts are nice.

Continue to blend add olive oil a bit at a
time to get the right consistence.

If too bitter add some fresh basil to taste.

Serve up spaghetti
Buon appetito!

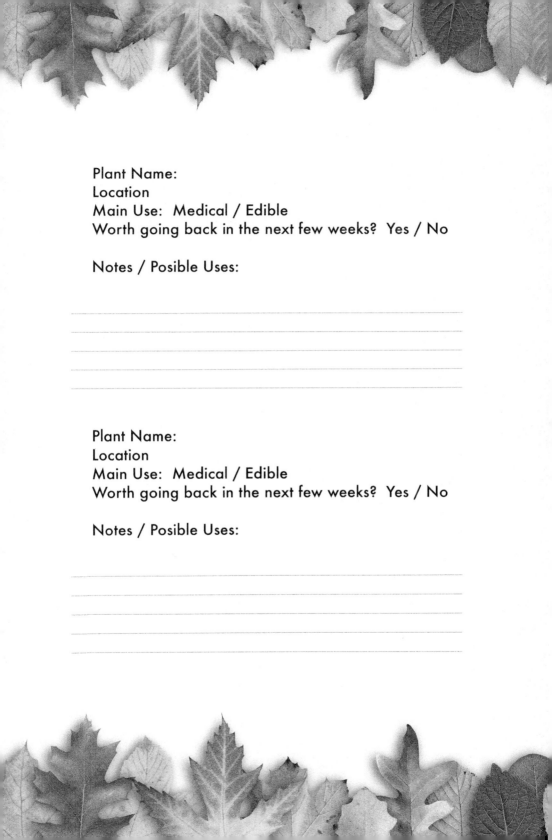

Plant Name:
Location
Main Use: Medical / Edible
Worth going back in the next few weeks? Yes / No

Notes / Posible Uses:

Plant Name:
Location
Main Use: Medical / Edible
Worth going back in the next few weeks? Yes / No

Notes / Posible Uses:

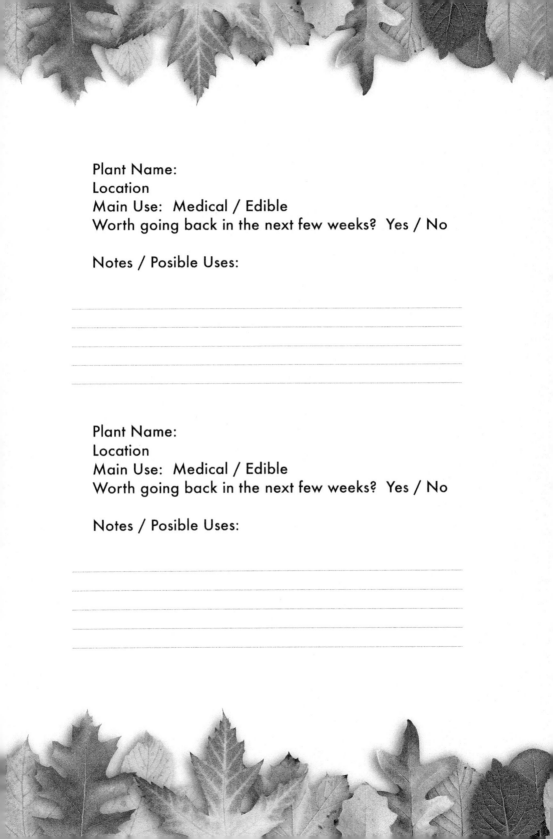

Plant Name:
Location
Main Use: Medical / Edible
Worth going back in the next few weeks? Yes / No

Notes / Posible Uses:

Plant Name:
Location
Main Use: Medical / Edible
Worth going back in the next few weeks? Yes / No

Notes / Posible Uses:

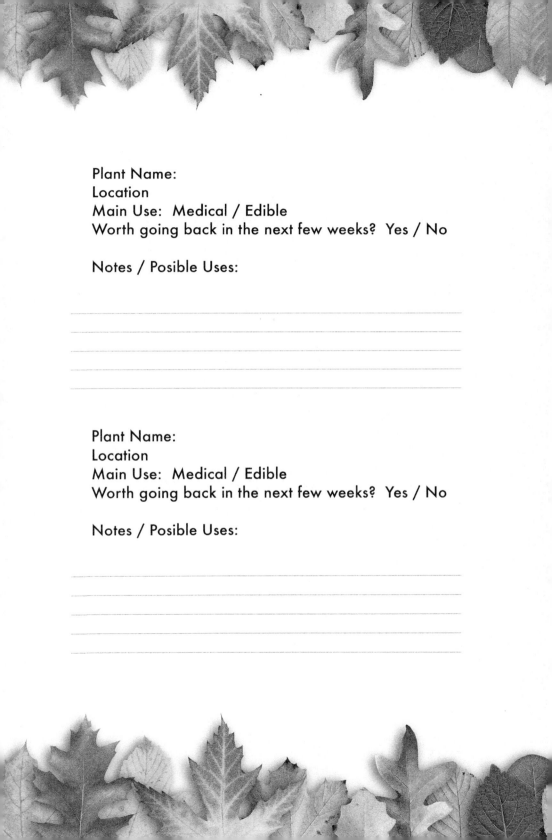

Plant Name:
Location
Main Use: Medical / Edible
Worth going back in the next few weeks? Yes / No

Notes / Posible Uses:

Plant Name:
Location
Main Use: Medical / Edible
Worth going back in the next few weeks? Yes / No

Notes / Posible Uses:

Taraxacum

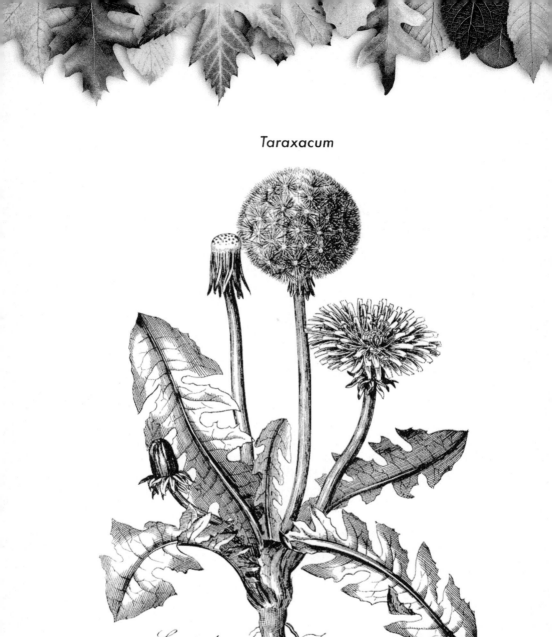

MARCH

Dandelion Chips
Taraxacum

Random Fact
The common name comes from the French Dent de Lion meaning lions tooth referring to the serrated teeth of the leaf.

Harvest
Make sure you have the right plant by the leaf and flower. If unsure wait for the flowers to come which will make the ID much easier.

Take both the leaf and the flower buds both are nice. You can also take the flower to make a tea from.

Ingredients
Olive Oil
Garlic
Hard Cheese
Chilli flakes

MARCH

Method
Break large bits of the leaf into a bowl.

Lightly oil and coat the leaves in the bowl.

Spread onto a baking tray making sure they do not touch.

Bake on high heat for 15 mins.

Season with grated cheese, chilli and salt.

Serve up with a movie!
Buon appetito!

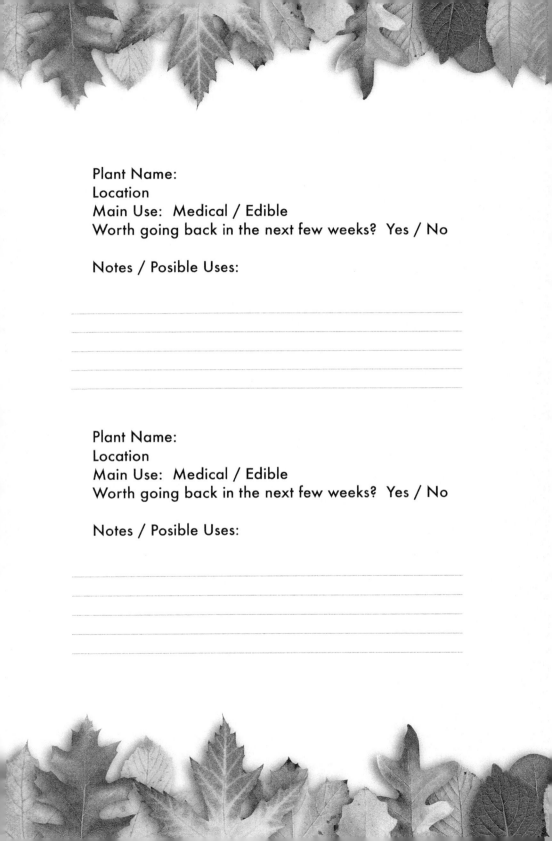

Plant Name:
Location
Main Use: Medical / Edible
Worth going back in the next few weeks? Yes / No

Notes / Posible Uses:

Plant Name:
Location
Main Use: Medical / Edible
Worth going back in the next few weeks? Yes / No

Notes / Posible Uses:

Plant Name:
Location
Main Use: Medical / Edible
Worth going back in the next few weeks? Yes / No

Notes / Posible Uses:

Plant Name:
Location
Main Use: Medical / Edible
Worth going back in the next few weeks? Yes / No

Notes / Posible Uses:

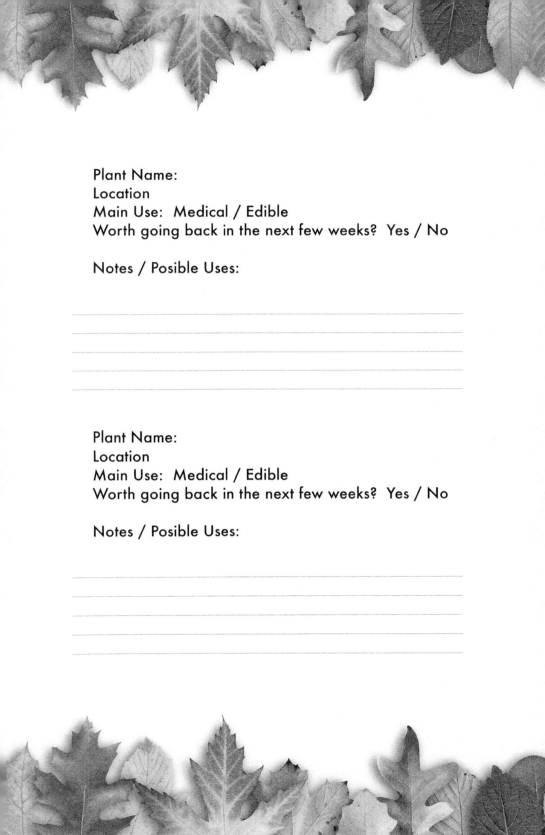

Plant Name:
Location
Main Use: Medical / Edible
Worth going back in the next few weeks? Yes / No

Notes / Posible Uses:

Plant Name:
Location
Main Use: Medical / Edible
Worth going back in the next few weeks? Yes / No

Notes / Posible Uses:

Urtica dioica

APRIL

Nettle Soup
Urtica dioica

Random Fact
The Roman's medical use for nettle was to strike themselves on the back as a cure for back pain... I have not tried this yet!

Harvest
Use gloves unless you are brave (rubber gloves are fine) Long sleeves are also a good idea. Collect the fresh top four leaves of the nettles . One bags worth is a normal amount and will take you 5 minutes.

Cooking will remove the sting... I promise!

Ingredient
Olive Oil
Onion
Garlic
Potatoes
Carrots
Any spare "soup" vegetables

APRIL

Method

Fry onion on low heat for 5 minutes.

Add cut squared potatoes and carrots.

Any other soup vegetables.

Add stock water to cover vegetables.

After 15 mins add nettles... carefully

Add Chilli or curry spices to your liking.

After 5 minutes more cooking use a hand blender to liquidise.

Serve up with parmesan cheese
Buon appetito!

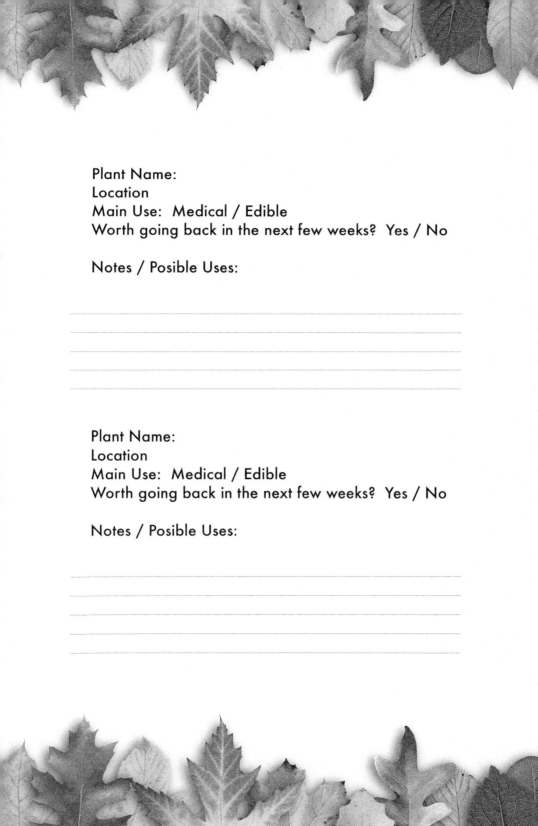

Plant Name:
Location
Main Use: Medical / Edible
Worth going back in the next few weeks? Yes / No

Notes / Posible Uses:

Plant Name:
Location
Main Use: Medical / Edible
Worth going back in the next few weeks? Yes / No

Notes / Posible Uses:

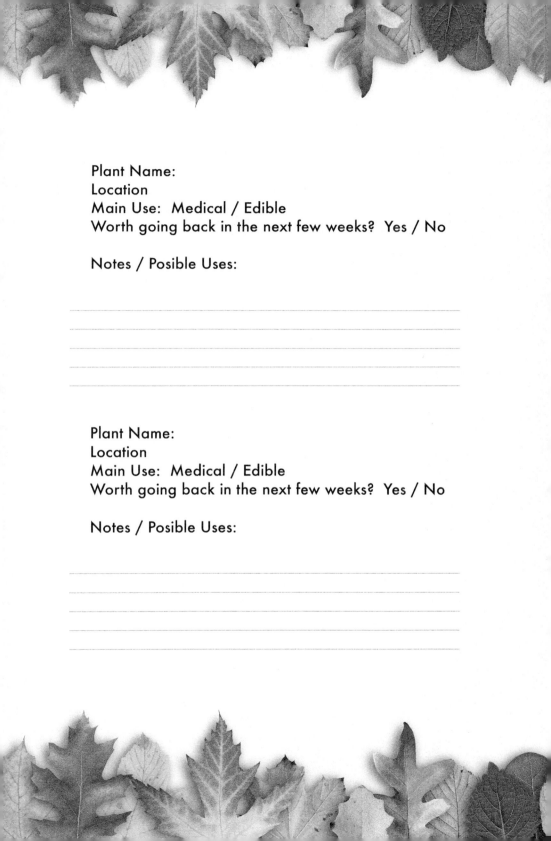

Plant Name:
Location
Main Use: Medical / Edible
Worth going back in the next few weeks? Yes / No

Notes / Posible Uses:

Plant Name:
Location
Main Use: Medical / Edible
Worth going back in the next few weeks? Yes / No

Notes / Posible Uses:

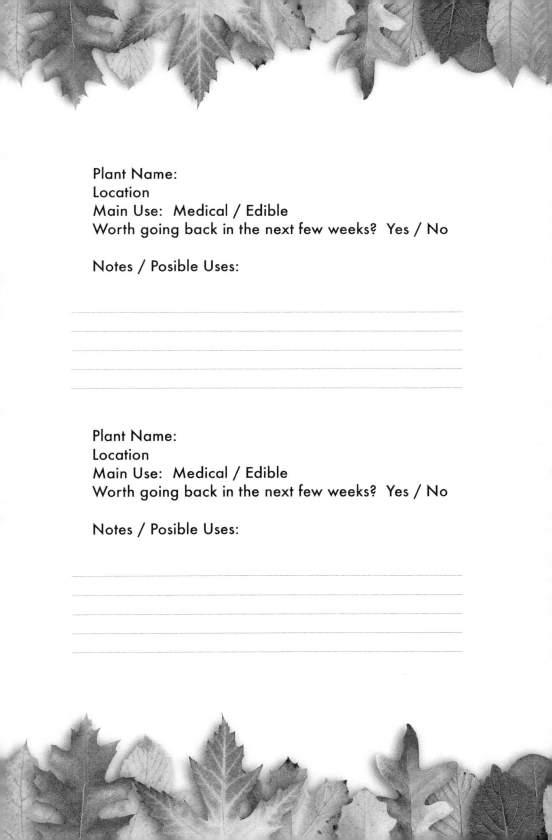

Plant Name:
Location
Main Use: Medical / Edible
Worth going back in the next few weeks? Yes / No

Notes / Posible Uses:

Plant Name:
Location
Main Use: Medical / Edible
Worth going back in the next few weeks? Yes / No

Notes / Posible Uses:

Plant Name:
Location
Main Use: Medical / Edible
Worth going back in the next few weeks? Yes / No

Notes / Posible Uses:

Plant Name:
Location
Main Use: Medical / Edible
Worth going back in the next few weeks? Yes / No

Notes / Posible Uses:

Allium ursinum

MAY

Wild Garlic with Boiled Egg
Allium ursinum

Simple but amazing way to uplight
a normal breakfast.

Random Fact
Has as much if not more health benefits
as "normal" garlic like lowering
blood pressure.

Harvest
Fresh Leaves
Check smell before taking
(should smell strongly of garlic)

Ingredient
Eggs Free range of course!
Butter

MAY

Method

Boil some water in a pan.

Add egg for 4 minutes.

Shred wild garlic leaves on to buttered toast.

Serve up with homemade toast
Buon appetito!

Plant Name:
Location
Main Use: Medical / Edible
Worth going back in the next few weeks? Yes / No

Notes / Posible Uses:

Plant Name:
Location
Main Use: Medical / Edible
Worth going back in the next few weeks? Yes / No

Notes / Posible Uses:

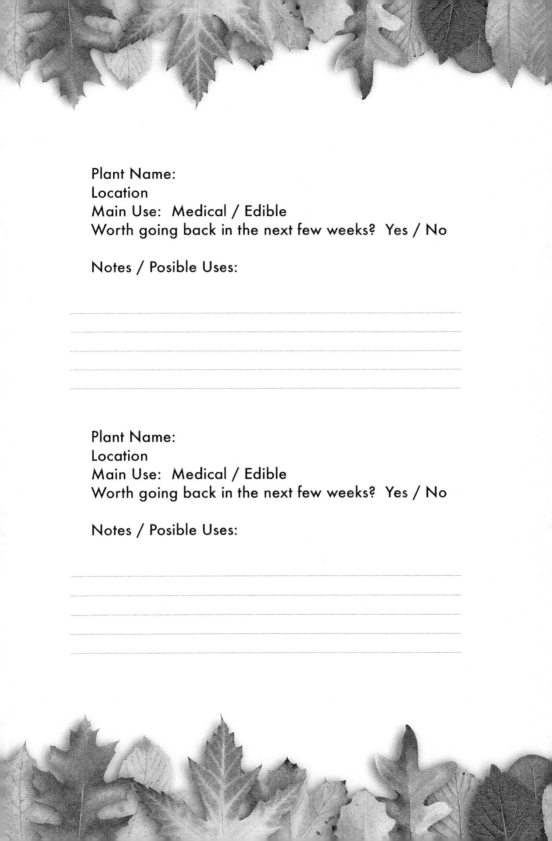

Plant Name:
Location
Main Use: Medical / Edible
Worth going back in the next few weeks? Yes / No

Notes / Posible Uses:

Plant Name:
Location
Main Use: Medical / Edible
Worth going back in the next few weeks? Yes / No

Notes / Posible Uses:

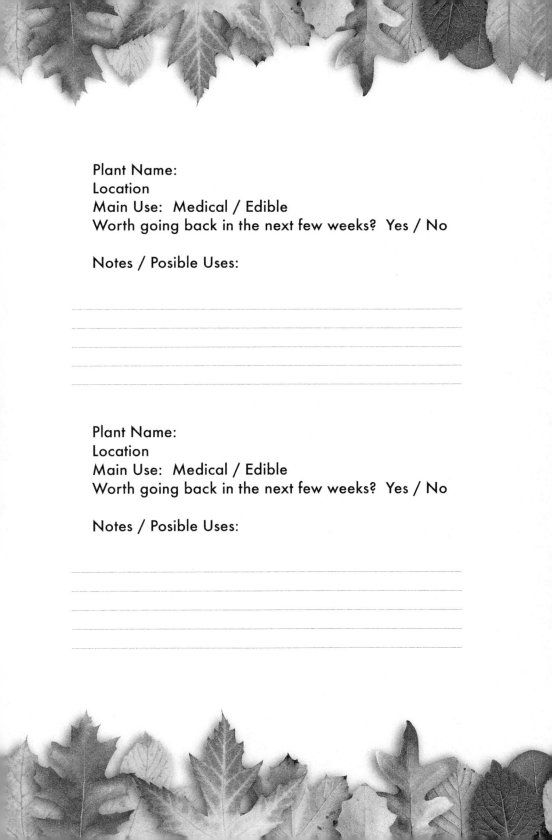

Plant Name:
Location
Main Use: Medical / Edible
Worth going back in the next few weeks? Yes / No

Notes / Posible Uses:

Plant Name:
Location
Main Use: Medical / Edible
Worth going back in the next few weeks? Yes / No

Notes / Posible Uses:

Sambucus

Pl.150. Sureau noir. Sambucus nigra L.

JUNE

Elderflower Cordial
Sambucus

Random Fact
Common name come from the Anglo-Saxon "aeld" which means fire as the stems are hollow and used as bellows for a fire.

Harvest
20 Fresh flower stalks
Wash flowers to remove insects

Ingredient
Water
Sugar
Lemons
Bottles
Sterile bottles

Sterile bottles
Place clean bottles in a large saucepan add enough water to cover boil rapidly for 5 minutes.

JUNE

Method

Boil 2 Litres of water.

Add 2Kg sugar and dissolve sugar.

Add 3 lemons and bits of lemon zest, avoid the white pith as it will make, the drink bitter.

Strain and bottle into sterile bottles.

Use within two weeks.

Serve up with fizzy water
Buon appetito!

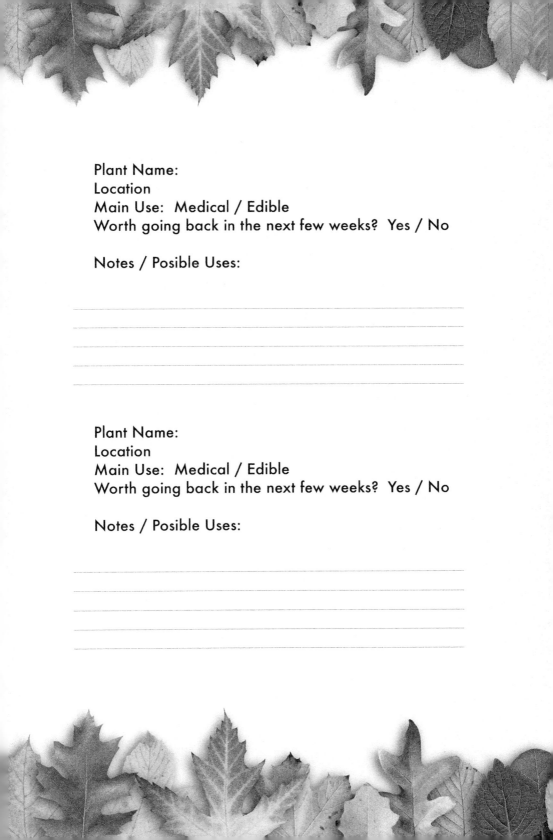

Plant Name:
Location
Main Use: Medical / Edible
Worth going back in the next few weeks? Yes / No

Notes / Posible Uses:

Plant Name:
Location
Main Use: Medical / Edible
Worth going back in the next few weeks? Yes / No

Notes / Posible Uses:

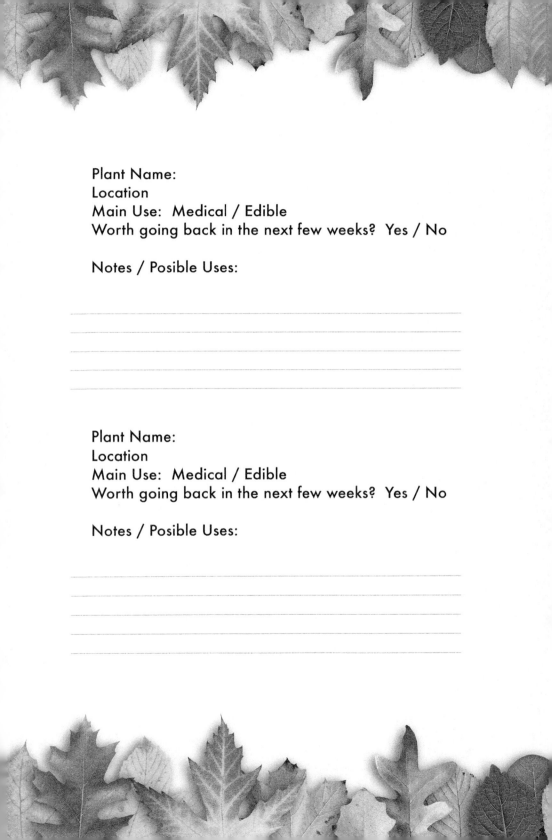

Plant Name:
Location
Main Use: Medical / Edible
Worth going back in the next few weeks? Yes / No

Notes / Posible Uses:

_____
_____
_____
_____
_____

Plant Name:
Location
Main Use: Medical / Edible
Worth going back in the next few weeks? Yes / No

Notes / Posible Uses:

_____
_____
_____
_____
_____

Plant Name:
Location
Main Use: Medical / Edible
Worth going back in the next few weeks? Yes / No

Notes / Posible Uses:

_____
_____
_____
_____
_____

Plant Name:
Location
Main Use: Medical / Edible
Worth going back in the next few weeks? Yes / No

Notes / Posible Uses:

_____
_____
_____
_____
_____

Filipendula ulmaria

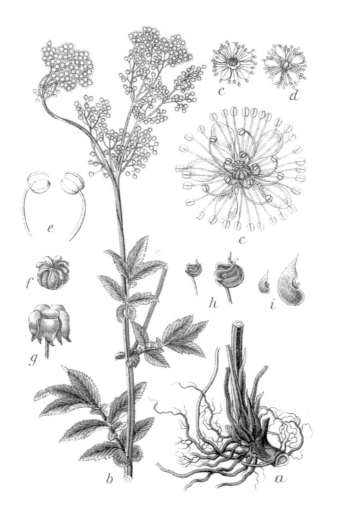

JULY

Meadowsweet and strawberry smoothie
Filipendula ulmaria

Tiny, creamy-white flowers growing on reddish stems. They can grow 1-2 meter tall in meadows.

Random Fact
Contains salicylic acid and was the plant that aspirin was derived from.

Harvest
2 flower stalks

More if you want to make a cordial as for elderflower recipe.

Ingredients
Wild strawberries
Meadowsweet flowers
Milk
Yogurt

JULY

Method
Throw flower minus stalks into a blender with the strawberries.

Add 1 cup of milk and 1/2 cup of yogurt.

Add a few cubes of ice.

Blend!

Serve on its own!
Buon appetito!

Plant Name:
Location
Main Use: Medical / Edible
Worth going back in the next few weeks? Yes / No

Notes / Posible Uses:

_____
_____
_____
_____

Plant Name:
Location
Main Use: Medical / Edible
Worth going back in the next few weeks? Yes / No

Notes / Posible Uses:

_____
_____
_____
_____

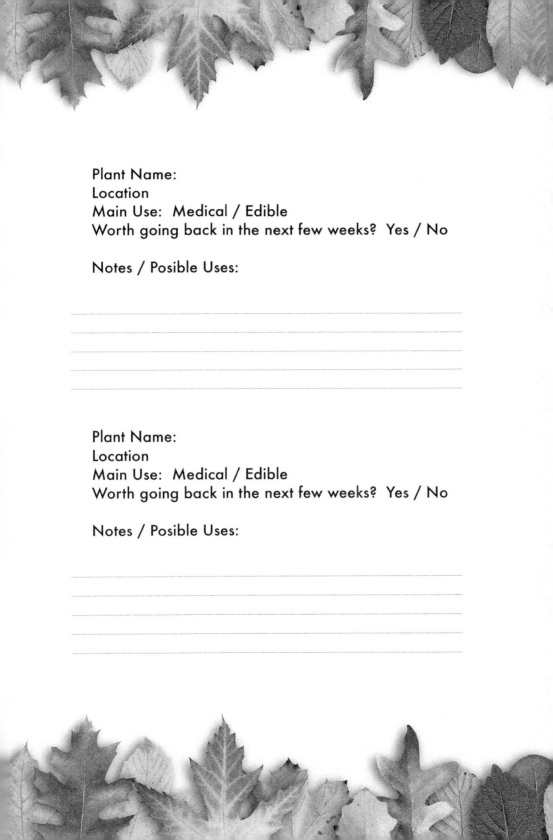

Plant Name:
Location
Main Use: Medical / Edible
Worth going back in the next few weeks? Yes / No

Notes / Posible Uses:

Plant Name:
Location
Main Use: Medical / Edible
Worth going back in the next few weeks? Yes / No

Notes / Posible Uses:

Plant Name:
Location
Main Use: Medical / Edible
Worth going back in the next few weeks? Yes / No

Notes / Posible Uses:

Plant Name:
Location
Main Use: Medical / Edible
Worth going back in the next few weeks? Yes / No

Notes / Posible Uses:

Filipendula ulmaria

Pl.150. Sureau noir. Sambucus nigra L.

AUGUST

Elderberry Flu Stopping Jelly
Filipendula ulmaria

Random Fact
A constituent of the Elderberry surrounds the flu virus and stops it invading or cells.

Harvest
Pick whole stalk

Use a fork to "de" berries back at home.

Ingredients
Lemon
Sugar

Sterile Jars
Place clean jars in a large saucepan add enough water to cover boil rapidly for 5 minutes.

AUGUST

Method

Equal amounts sugar to berries.

A few cups of water.

Juice of one lemon.

Tie some lemon seeds in a piece of cheesecloth and simmer that
with your jelly

(Acts as a natural pectin).

Add to jars.

Serve with game meat!
Buon appetito!

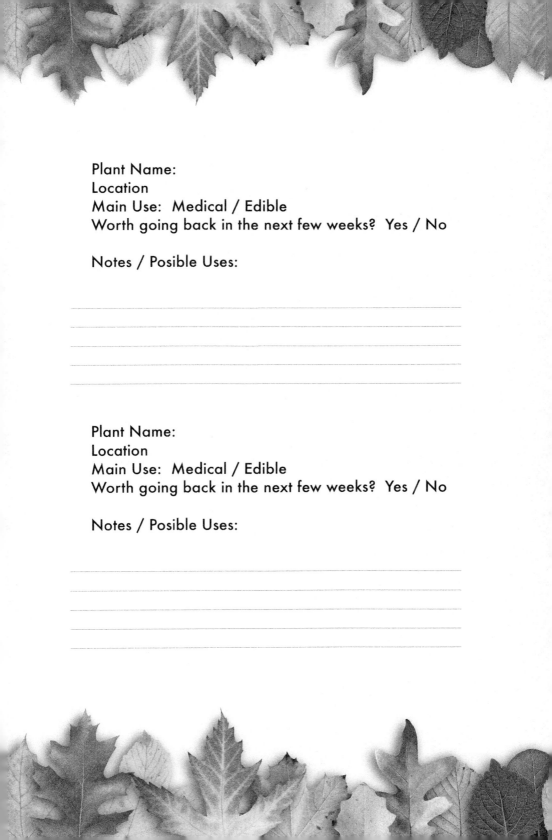

Plant Name:
Location
Main Use: Medical / Edible
Worth going back in the next few weeks? Yes / No

Notes / Posible Uses:

Plant Name:
Location
Main Use: Medical / Edible
Worth going back in the next few weeks? Yes / No

Notes / Posible Uses:

Plant Name:
Location
Main Use: Medical / Edible
Worth going back in the next few weeks? Yes / No

Notes / Posible Uses:

_____
_____
_____
_____
_____

Plant Name:
Location
Main Use: Medical / Edible
Worth going back in the next few weeks? Yes / No

Notes / Posible Uses:

_____
_____
_____
_____
_____

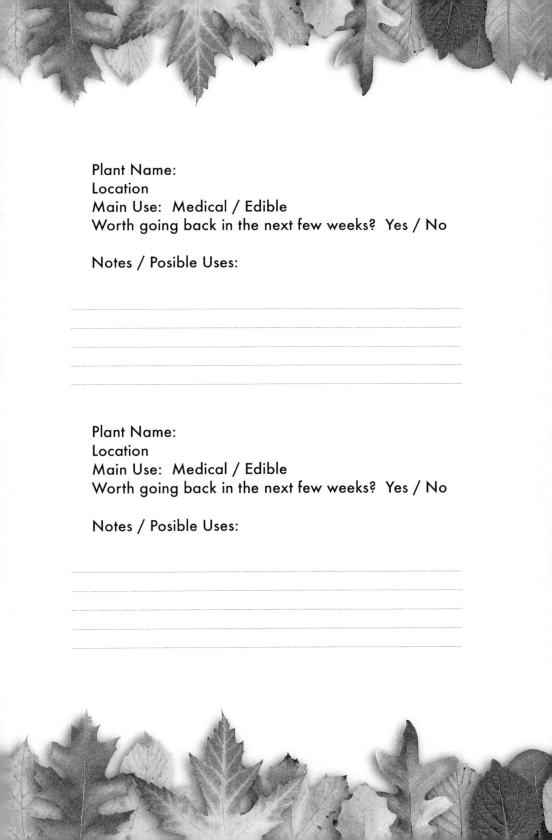

Plant Name:
Location
Main Use: Medical / Edible
Worth going back in the next few weeks? Yes / No

Notes / Posible Uses:

Plant Name:
Location
Main Use: Medical / Edible
Worth going back in the next few weeks? Yes / No

Notes / Posible Uses:

Prunus spinosa

SEPTEMBER

Blackthorn Gin (Sloe Gin)
Prunus spinosa

If you can't find blackthorn then use a native plum.

Random Fact
Wood was used in the traditional Irish cudgel or shillelagh

Harvest
Wait for first frost as this sweetens the fruit slightly.

500g Blue-black fruits measuring 1cm across

Watch the thorns!

Ingredients
500g of sloes
250g of sugar
1 Bottle of gin
1 Empty bottle of gin

SEPTEMBER

Method
Freeze sloes overnight, as this helps to split the skins.

Empty sloes into two empty gin bottles.

Add 250g of sugar.

Store and shake when you remember.

Save and serve up at Christmas.

Serve with stilton or a mixer to fizz
Buon appetito!

Plant Name:
Location
Main Use: Medical / Edible
Worth going back in the next few weeks? Yes / No

Notes / Posible Uses:

_____
_____
_____
_____

Plant Name:
Location
Main Use: Medical / Edible
Worth going back in the next few weeks? Yes / No

Notes / Posible Uses:

_____
_____
_____
_____

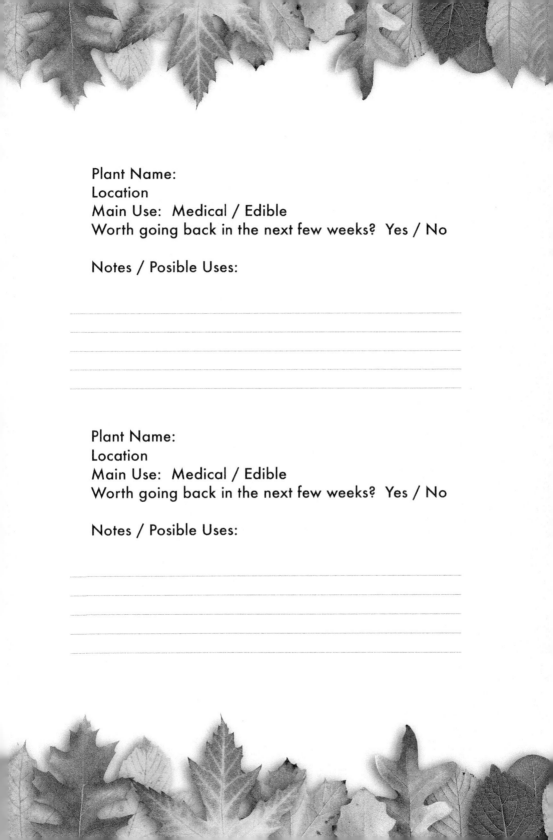

Plant Name:
Location
Main Use: Medical / Edible
Worth going back in the next few weeks? Yes / No

Notes / Posible Uses:

Plant Name:
Location
Main Use: Medical / Edible
Worth going back in the next few weeks? Yes / No

Notes / Posible Uses:

Plant Name:
Location
Main Use: Medical / Edible
Worth going back in the next few weeks? Yes / No

Notes / Posible Uses:

_____
_____
_____
_____
_____

Plant Name:
Location
Main Use: Medical / Edible
Worth going back in the next few weeks? Yes / No

Notes / Posible Uses:

_____
_____
_____
_____
_____

Corylus avellana

OCTOBER

Hazelnut Chocolate
Corylus avellana

Random Fact
Traditionally cut for its long straight sticks for fences, plant supports and walking sticks.

Harvest
2 cups of hazelnuts. When the papery covering starts pulling back from the nut then they should be edible.
Good luck in beating the wildlife.
You can pick green and allow them to "ripen"

Ingredients
1/4 cup sugar
1 pound of chocolate
1/2 cup of butter
Bottle of cream

Sterile Jars
Place clean jars in a large saucepan and add enough water to cover boil rapidly for 5 minutes.

OCTOBER

Method
Grind hazelnuts and 1/4 cup sugar
in a blender.

Melt 1 pound of chocolate and
1/2 cup of butter.

Add a pinch of salt and a bottle of cream.

Add hazelnut powder.

Mix and add to jars.

Serve with French pancakes
Buon appetito!

Plant Name:
Location
Main Use: Medical / Edible
Worth going back in the next few weeks? Yes / No

Notes / Posible Uses:

Plant Name:
Location
Main Use: Medical / Edible
Worth going back in the next few weeks? Yes / No

Notes / Posible Uses:

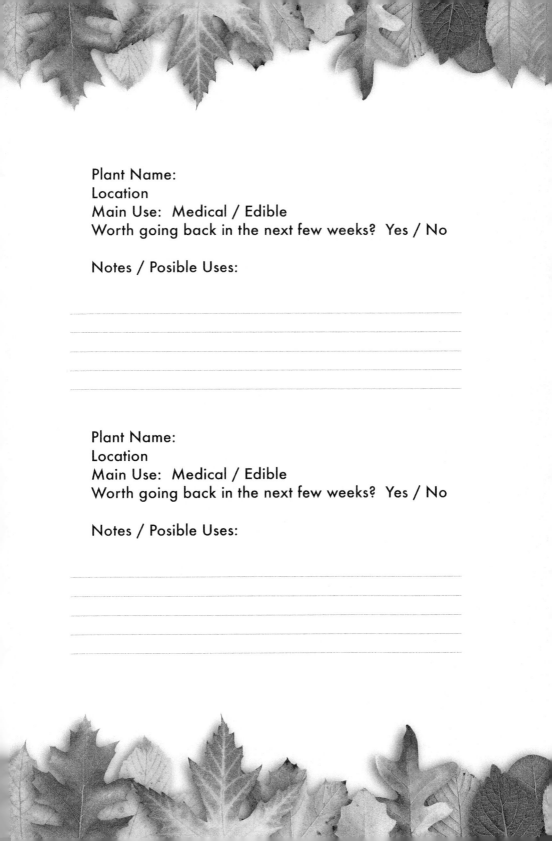

Plant Name:
Location
Main Use: Medical / Edible
Worth going back in the next few weeks? Yes / No

Notes / Posible Uses:

_____
_____
_____
_____
_____

Plant Name:
Location
Main Use: Medical / Edible
Worth going back in the next few weeks? Yes / No

Notes / Posible Uses:

_____
_____
_____
_____
_____

Plant Name:
Location
Main Use: Medical / Edible
Worth going back in the next few weeks? Yes / No

Notes / Posible Uses:

_____
_____
_____
_____
_____

Plant Name:
Location
Main Use: Medical / Edible
Worth going back in the next few weeks? Yes / No

Notes / Posible Uses:

_____
_____
_____
_____
_____

Sorbus Aucuparia

NOVEMBER

Rowan Jelly
Sorbus Aucuparia

Random Fact
In the middle ages Rowan was made into Bows.

Harvest
2 pounds of Rowan Berries
2 pounds of crab apples

Ingredients
2 pounds of Rowan Berries
2 pounds of crab apples
One cup of sugar

Sterile Jars
Place clean jar in a large saucepan and add enough water to cover boil rapidly for 5 minutes.

NOVEMBER

Method
Add chopped fruit to pan and half fill with water.

Boil and mash with large fork.

Add fruit to jelly bags and drain.

Add one cup of sugar for every cup of Juice.

Boil until setting point (sets on cold spoon).

Add to jars.

Serve with game or lamb
Buon appetito!

Plant Name:
Location
Main Use: Medical / Edible
Worth going back in the next few weeks? Yes / No

Notes / Posible Uses:

_____
_____
_____
_____
_____

Plant Name:
Location
Main Use: Medical / Edible
Worth going back in the next few weeks? Yes / No

Notes / Posible Uses:

_____
_____
_____
_____
_____

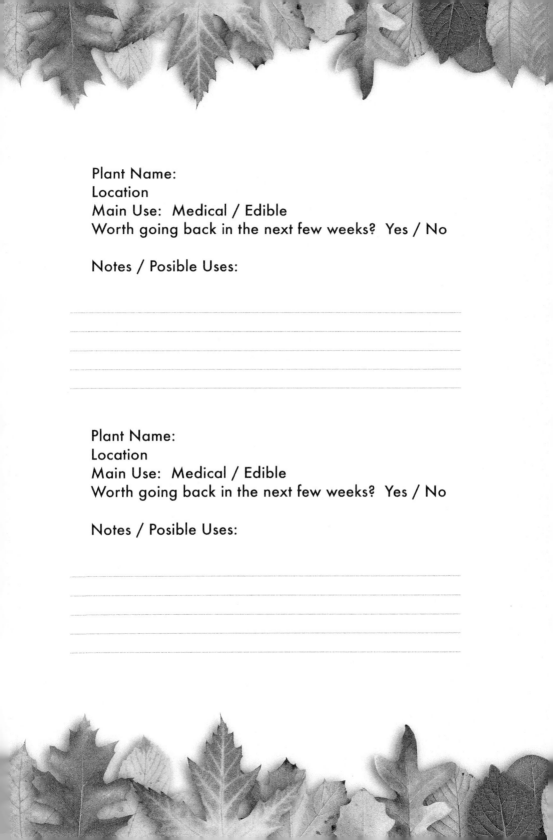

Plant Name:
Location
Main Use: Medical / Edible
Worth going back in the next few weeks? Yes / No

Notes / Posible Uses:

_____
_____
_____
_____
_____

Plant Name:
Location
Main Use: Medical / Edible
Worth going back in the next few weeks? Yes / No

Notes / Posible Uses:

_____
_____
_____
_____
_____

Plant Name:
Location
Main Use: Medical / Edible
Worth going back in the next few weeks? Yes / No

Notes / Posible Uses:

_____
_____
_____
_____
_____

Plant Name:
Location
Main Use: Medical / Edible
Worth going back in the next few weeks? Yes / No

Notes / Posible Uses:

_____
_____
_____
_____
_____

Rosa canina

DECEMBER

Rose Hip syrup
Rosa canina

Random Fact
In the second world war, children were employed to collect the hips for the war effort, as the high vitamin C was needed.

Harvest
2 pounds of hips

Ingredients
2 pounds of hips
2 pounds of sugar

Sterile bottles
Place clean bottles in a large saucepan add enough water to cover boil rapidly for 5 minutes.

DECEMBER

Method
Layer hips and sugar into bottles.

Repeat until you have run out
of bottles or hips.

Leave in a sunny spot and
turn every day.

Syrup will be drawn from the hips.

Drain into sterile bottles though fine cloth.

Serve with ice-cream
Buon appetito!

Plant Name:
Location
Main Use: Medical / Edible
Worth going back in the next few weeks? Yes / No

Notes / Posible Uses:

_____
_____
_____
_____
_____

Plant Name:
Location
Main Use: Medical / Edible
Worth going back in the next few weeks? Yes / No

Notes / Posible Uses:

_____
_____
_____
_____
_____

Plant Name:
Location
Main Use: Medical / Edible
Worth going back in the next few weeks? Yes / No

Notes / Posible Uses:

_____
_____
_____
_____
_____

Plant Name:
Location
Main Use: Medical / Edible
Worth going back in the next few weeks? Yes / No

Notes / Posible Uses:

_____
_____
_____
_____
_____

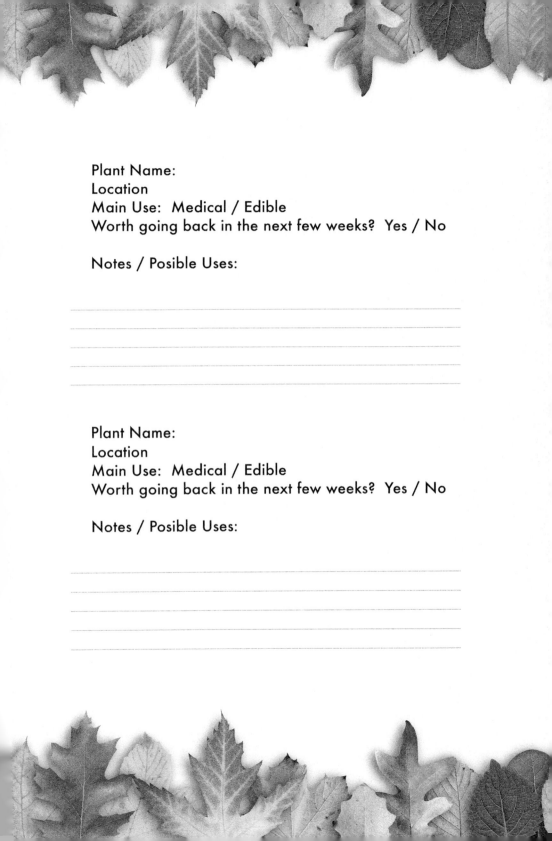

Plant Name:
Location
Main Use: Medical / Edible
Worth going back in the next few weeks? Yes / No

Notes / Posible Uses:

Plant Name:
Location
Main Use: Medical / Edible
Worth going back in the next few weeks? Yes / No

Notes / Posible Uses:

Printed in Great Britain
by Amazon